YOUR PASSPORT TO

CUBA

>> *by Ruth Manning* >>

CAPSTONE PRESS
a capstone imprint

Published by Capstone Press, an imprint of Capstone
1710 Roe Crest Drive, North Mankato, Minnesota 56003
capstonepub.com

Library of Congress Cataloging-in-Publication Data is available on the Library
of Congress website.
ISBN: 9781669058465 (hardcover)
ISBN: 9781669058410 (paperback)
ISBN: 9781669058427 (ebook PDF)

Summary: What is it like to live in or visit Cuba? What makes Cuba's culture
unique? Explore the geography, traditions, and daily lives of Cubans.

Editorial Credits
Editor: Carrie Sheely; Designer: Bobbie Nuytten; Media Researcher: Rebekah
Hubstenberger; Production Specialist: Whitney Schaefer

Image Credits
Alamy: Chronicle, 10, History and Art Collection, 29, Karol Kozlowski
Premium RM Collection, 14, Ron Giling, 25; Capstone Press: Eric Gohl, 5;
Getty Images: Grafissimo, 9, iStock/anzeletti, 15, Jorge Rey/Newsmakers, 12,
Keystone-France/Gamma-Keystone, 6, Nick Laham, 27, Roberto Machado Noa,
20; Shutterstock: akturer, 19, Anton_Ivanov, 16, bayazed, 8, Gil.K, 23, Kamira,
Cover (bottom), MIGUEL G. SAAVEDRA, 28

Design Elements
Getty Images: iStock/Yevhenii Dubinko; Shutterstock: Flipser, KASUE (map),
Net Vector, pingebat, Platinum Photographer (flag)

Capstone thanks Omar Granados, director of the University of Wisconsin-La
Crosse Institute for Latin American and Latino Studies, for sharing his expertise
during the production of this book.

All internet sites appearing in back matter were available and accurate when
this book was sent to press.

Printed and bound in China. PO 5593

CONTENTS

Words in **bold** are in the glossary.

CHAPTER ONE

WELCOME TO CUBA!

Old buildings surround a cobblestone square. In the center is a park filled with trees. People sit and chat on its benches. Around the edges, people set up stands. They will sell books, artwork, and souvenirs from the stands. A band plays salsa music. From nearby restaurants comes the smell of delicious food. This place is Plaza de Armas. It is in Cuba's capital city, Havana.

Cuba is an island country on the northern edge of the Caribbean Sea. About 11 million people live there. Cuba has natural beauty with forests, mountains, and beaches. It also has a long and colorful history. Its culture includes a mix of African and Spanish **traditions**.

MAP OF CUBA

Varadero

HAVANA — El Capitolio — Hicacos Peninsula

Viñales Valley — Plaza de Armas

Trinidad   **CUBA**

Santiago de Cuba

Sierra Maestra

- ■ Capital City
- ● City
- ⬡ Landform
- △ Landmark

N
W — E
S

Explore Cuba's cities
and landmarks.

CHAPTER TWO

HISTORY OF CUBA

Indigenous people lived in Cuba about 6,000 years ago. They hunted animals and gathered plants to eat. Later, other Indigenous people, including the Taíno, grew crops and fished. The Taíno made pottery and used stone tools. They lived in villages of up to 3,000 people. Their houses were called *bohíos*. They were made from natural materials such as palm leaves.

A rebuilt Taíno village in Cuba

EUROPEANS ARRIVE

Christopher Columbus came to Cuba in 1492. He was the first European to arrive. Soon, many more Europeans came. They built forts and towns. They **enslaved** the Indigenous people, making them work in mines and fields. Most of the Indigenous people soon died. Some died because of poor treatment. Others died from diseases that Europeans had brought. Their bodies couldn't defend against these diseases. The Europeans then enslaved people from Africa to work in Cuba.

FACT
||||||||||||||||||||||||||||||||||||||||||||||||||||

Sugarcane was once Cuba's most important crop. In 1860, Cuba produced one-third of the world's sugar. But it relied on the work of enslaved people to grow it.

Enslaved people from Africa harvest sugarcane in Cuba.

END OF SPANISH RULE

In the 1800s, some Cubans became unhappy with high taxes and other decisions the Spanish government made. A **revolution** to gain independence began in 1868. After 10 years, it failed.

Cuba's Spanish rulers finally banned slavery in 1886. But many Cubans wanted to rule themselves. Another revolution began in 1895.

Cuban revolutionary soldiers travel on horseback in the late 1890s.

The United States became involved in support of the Cubans. U.S. leaders feared the fight might disrupt trade with Cuba and other interests it had on the island. The Cubans won the war in 1898.

INDEPENDENCE

Cuba was independent. But U.S. forces stayed after defeating Spain in the Spanish-American War. It had control over Cuba's **economy**. In 1901, the U.S. made an agreement with Cuba called the Platt Amendment. It gave the U.S. the right to set up a naval base and to control parts of Cuba's government actions and economy. In 1902, the U.S. troops left Cuba.

Over time, conditions for Cubans declined. Many Cubans were poor, and the country's leaders didn't try to help. It was time for a change.

CITIES OLD AND NEW

Havana is Cuba's capital. It is also the largest city. It is on the northwest coast. Many of its buildings are very old. Built in the 1700s and 1800s, they have a Spanish style.

Colorful buildings line a street in Havana.

Havana is a lively city. There are large plazas with cafés and restaurants. Bands play live music, and people walk along the seafront. From 1929 to 1959, Cuba's congress met at El Capitolio in Havana. This building looks a lot like the U.S. Capitol in Washington, D.C.

Santiago de Cuba is on the southeast coast. This city is a mix of old and new. Museums tell the story of Castro's revolution. An old Spanish fortress overlooks the city. It is perched on a cliff. The city also has modern office buildings and hotels.

Trinidad has an old-fashioned feel. Fancy mansions line the cobblestone streets. Trinidad is famous for local crafts that are sold there. They include needlework and lace. Tourists shop and eat at open-air markets.

FIRST TOWN

Baracoa is Cuba's oldest city. The Spanish founded it in 1511. The city is near Cuba's eastern tip. The road leading there winds through beautiful mountain scenery.

CHAPTER FOUR

DAILY LIFE

Cuba is a socialist country. The government controls many aspects of daily life. It sets prices and gives out food. It runs the health care system.

Until recently, people couldn't own property. Many types of private businesses weren't allowed. Many people have left the country. They didn't agree with the government's control.

More than half of Cubans are Christians, and most of these are Catholic. Many Cubans follow a religion called Santeria. It is based on West African beliefs.

SCHOOL

The government runs the school system. School is free. All children must go until the age of 15 or 16. They wear uniforms.

Schoolchildren attend class in Trinidad.

CHAPTER SIX

SPORTS AND RECREATION

Sports are important in Cuba. The government wants everyone to take part. Sports centers are free to use. Children learn sports at school. Those with talent are involved in sports schools. They get training and support. For a small country, Cuba does well at the Olympics.

Baseball is the most popular sport. Cuba has produced many top players. Their national team has won more Olympic gold medals than any other country. But players are paid very little. Some move to the United States to play.

People play other sports in Cuba too. Boxing is a popular sport. Cuban boxers often win Olympic medals. Many people play volleyball and basketball. Cubans have also had success in track and field.

Cuba's Olympic baseball team celebrates after winning the gold medal in 2004.

INDEX

SELECT BOOKS IN THIS SERIES

YOUR PASSPORT TO **AUSTRALIA**
YOUR PASSPORT TO **BRAZIL**
YOUR PASSPORT TO **CANADA**
YOUR PASSPORT TO **ENGLAND**
YOUR PASSPORT TO **GERMANY**

YOUR PASSPORT TO **JAPAN**
YOUR PASSPORT TO **MEXICO**
YOUR PASSPORT TO **PORTUGAL**
YOUR PASSPORT TO **SAUDI ARABIA**
YOUR PASSPORT TO **SOUTH AFRICA**